The
HELPMATE

The
HELPMATE

By
Stephen B. Oladipo

ARPress
ILLUMINATING IDEAS.
EMPOWERING VOICES.

ARPress
45 Dan Road Suite 5
Canton, MA 02021

Hotline: 1(888) 821-0229
Fax: 1(508) 545-7580

Ordering Information:
Quantity sales. Special discounts are available on quantity purchases by corporations,associations, and others. For details, contact the publisher at the address above.

Printed in the United States of America.

ISBN-13:   Softcover   979-8-89356-548-5
            eBook   979-8-89356-549-2

Library of Congress Control Number: 2024902575

TABLE OF CONTENTS

ABOUT THE BOOK

This is a well-orchestrated prose-work, fiction. Although events in the narratives are mirrored to reflect real life occurences. It is a tragic story. A tale of struggles, hardship, fortune, survival and death. The Book has fifteen chapters in total running into 108 pages with intriguing starting and ending narratives which qualifies the story as a comical tragedy.

It touches on some cultural demeanors of people from certain tribes in Africa (Nigeria as a focus) where extra-marital affair is silently prevalent despite legality to engage in polygamy. The book: Helpmate muckrakes the evil of broken-homes and parental neglegence on young adults. The strenous roles of fending for self as a child and taking up the responsibility of an adult in the process of survival is pivotal incident within the pages.

Man's love for beast is not always without the influence of what they could produce. This statement is justified by the roles the Dog: 'Riro' plays on Dara's path to fulfilment. These unique roles have usually been sanctioned to be the reason why many pet-owners (especially in africa) own their Dogs and cater for them and not really because of unaligning love for these animals. The story justifies this more with the dramatic risk of life efforts 'Riro' (the Dog) had to make to preserve Dara's life while the Dog owner-Dara could not be said to attempt similar efforts to the turn of substituting his own life to rescue the Dog when her own (the Dog's) critical situation beckoned.

We dream, we hope, we expect with longings in life, but we do not know what tomorrow holds. This is explained by the unexpected and sudden end of Riro. For this sudden and unexpected end of Dara's lover bring him back to a zero level of fulfillment, bruising his desires like the impact of the sun upon a fallen leave ...

ABOUT THE AUTHOR

Dr. Stephen B. Oladipo is a policy analyst, a trained journalist, an educator and a certified investigator. As a research-expert, he has served severally as a team-member in some of World Health Organization (WHO)'s research projects in Africa. He has been a research committee-member in many UNICEF, UNFPA and Population Council's research projects in Nigeria, Africa.

As a scholar, he is well published with about twenty-two (22) educational books aside international journals to his credit. Some of his books have once been approved for use within the school system in his country of origin. To recognise his immense contributions to prose and poetry, he won the Editor's choice awards with International Library of Congress 2007 and 2008 back to back.

He attained a Doctorate degree in Criminology with specialty on insurgence-diagnosis. His decade plus experience as a security-agent equally contributed immensely to his depth of understanding in security related matters.

His works are available and accessible globally through the major online retailers such as Amazon, eBay, barnes&nobles and numerous other book stores.

He is currently advancing his career within the borders of the United States of America.

DEDICATED TO MY SIBLINGS,

IN THE MEMORY OF OUR DAD

AND OUR DOGS.

TO CONSOLE THE MEN OF ILL-OMEN.

IT'S ABOUT THE UPS

AND DOWNS OF LIFE.

PROLOGUE

This is about the fate, the root and the chances of survival of the Ordinary Nigerian Children like that of others in the region of Africa.

FROM THE AFRICANS' CRADLE

It was dawn.

The birth of a new day;

As fresh as a daisy.

Hail! To the precious gift,

A fruit of the womb.

Patter of feet,

Bang of doors.

The more dancing

The many joke-ovation of the populace,

Expressed the joy of being born

Rather than the unplanned future;

The empty hope of survival

A head the implicated, innocent laddie;

Who emerged the tenth child

Under the thatch of the peasant.

Now! Another child has come into the country:

One of the many countries,

Technologically backwards,

One of the indigent countries;

A country in the third world category.

Having less than 30 percent chances

To survive the killer diseases;
The inevitable symptoms of the infancy.

Right into an unclean environment,

With no clean water.

Inadequate medical services;

Where the few doctors available,

Have few facilities at their disposal.

He took pains crawling in the sands,

Feeding on carbohydrate

Starch foods on the daily basis

The desire to school is beget.

Hence, serious odds to battle against;

The dormant brain to pep. And

Despite no assured means,

The obligations must be paid for,

Out of the meager pennies;

A token, gathered from great strain.

Now, with the many wants:

The immediate needs and the fees

Suppressed the minute income;

For the peasant boast of no asset,

Living from hand to mouth.

Government came to extricate,

Offering free education

To the awaiting thousands;

The many dawdle heads,

Exceeding the available facilities;

Making teaching difficult for the available hands.

Hence, the learners are compressed,

Jammed in the poorly equipped classrooms.

Clearly unkempt environment;

Weedy and unattractive.

So, failure rates are high

Thus, growing persistently higher.

Schooling is rather taunted,

Many learners become dropouts

Rigours, labour continues;

What an endless struggle!

Rest says the toiler.

But man must struggle to survive;

From the cradle to the grave.

Stephen B. Oladipo

PREFACE

The helpmate is a fiction, though, reflecting real life event. It is a tragic story. A tale of struggles, hardship, fortune, survival and death.

Indiscipline inspires a wreck; Papa who places no value on his life gives extension a hand to experience a crash of matrimony. As through nonchalant attitude and moral degeneration, he despises his wife for a reasonable while, playing harlotry under the shelter of a prostitute, which results in the divorce between him and the wife.

It stands a fact therefore that when the heavens refuse to rain, it is the ground that suffers. This is the more reason Dara suffers hardship and much more of loneliness and dejection than necessary, as this is not unconnected to this departure of his mother.

Man's love for beast is not always without the influence of what they could produce. Dara, dearly loves Riro but twice to deny the beast of the commensurate action as the proof of this love, even, when Riro chooses to risk her life in his rescue, Dara in returns chooses to pay her with pity from a distance.

We dream, we hope, we expect with longings in life, but we do not know what tomorrow holds. This is explained by the unexpected and sudden end of Riro. For this sudden and unexpected end of Dara's lover bring him back to a zero level of fulfillment, bruising his desires like the impact of the sun upon a fallen leave ...

CHAPTER 1

Encircled with the strain of negligence, he projected the will to surpass history. Lightening was never meant to strike twice in the same place. Reverse was the order in this respect. There was a crash of thunder, then, the storm struck. The quest to survive hit the rock bottom. The innocent laddie felt the pinch, fending for life in the region of indigence.

The difficulties obviously approached a climax when the poor papa's death became pronounced. The brilliant sun declined to shine. Paleness bothered the sky. Life in its entirety made no more meanings than the beginning of an end. Wearable surroundings. The lookers-on loitered compassion; it was Papa's interment. Everyone was not in tears because Papa was dead, but for this boy. How would Dara survive? How would he sustain himself? How would he continue his education? These were issues, locked in the secret of time and chances.

Papa had lived in straitened circumstances some few years before his death. It did not agree however that Papa never experienced wealth in the course of life, but he was a flirt. He chased strange women around and lavished money on them. Whenever Papa saw anything in skirt, his problems were over. He could sacrifice anything just to satisfy his lust, even to the detriment of his immediate family. While he was in money, his household still suffered. Sometime, he had evacuated his home for a resettlement with a harlot who harbored him like a bride. He was under the spell of this woman for several years before he came to his senses. This was a belated realization. The abandonment aided his wife leaving him for another man. She left to return never. Hence, his chamber was as open as the gate of hell. It was as accommodating as a restaurant. Several women trooped in night and day, winter and summer. All for a purpose, his money was their target. Papa was as graceful as roses in his youthful days. Only that he worn himself out through over extra sexual activity. He looked haggard, older than his age before his death. His dilapidated body disfigured him as he advanced in years. Though, that did not debar his adulterous partners coming for his money until Papa's resource was spent out.

The house he lived in was made of mud; it was inherited. There was nothing spectacular in Papa's parlor than a set of three old cushion-chairs, a table, a cabinet and an inherited little television set. He attached much value to this electronics that none in his household was permitted to put it on in his absence. He was the only operator. He could not entrust it in care of any other member of his immediate family, for fear of damage. He didn't subscribe to frivolous spending. Hence, he switched it on and off at his pleasure. The only appearance of significance in his bedroom was the working bunk. This couch served its purpose well in Papa's active days. It was on it that Papa wrestled with the women of his like passion.

The funniest was the fact that the mattress on this bed was not his. Papa snatched it from a sojourner who came to squat under his roof sometime ago. If not, Papa would have continued to lie on a bare clothed springs.

Many of his kindred had deserted him when his style of living was not compatible with theirs. Some of them regarded him as a bastard in the family. On several occasions they talked this to his face but papa showed no concern. Since he was an easygoing man, he made no trouble with any of them. Rather, he left them to the opinion of theirs. Nevertheless it was an open secret that Papa died of venereal diseases.

That was the point his condition became critical, demanding medical attention. But then, the wheel of fortune no longer spun in his favour. The old man could hardly fend for himself. He couldn't even find the euphoria of the past glory to live on. Virtually, everything was gone: the strength, the connections and friends. There was nothing to fall back on. Hence, he strove to make ends meet. Though he had begun to realize many of his past mistakes such as leaving his flesh and blood un-catered for. He had also begun to make effort, depriving himself of certain pleasure to pay-up his child's school-bills. This de-emphasized the fact that he had begun to better his lackadaisical approach to parenting his son. After all, that was the only boy he was left with, since he could no longer derive pleasure in the shadows of recklessness.

His death at this time was consequently unfortunate to Dara. Papa had died untimely, no legacy, no family. There was neither friend nor sure kin-men who could take up the burial responsibilities. It was option less; he would have to be buried wretchedly. Yet this could not amount to how Dara was going to survive. Although the boy has acquainted himself with petty jobs as clearing bushes around other people's houses. He also fetched water for others. At other times, he ran errands for neighboring families, right before he advanced into puberty. He usually accumulated such wages to complement the little money Papa gave to him. Nevertheless, the parental contribution was indispensable to his survival. Of course, this has been sustaining him. Not to mention now, when such was more necessary if he must further his education. It was worth therefore to justify the young man's view of life. He has often opined that life has never been emotional in his situation. Somehow at one point or the other in the formation of his advancement, troubles of greater magnitude emerged to discomfit his spirit. This has plagued his effort conscientiously. Just like the discharge of the Nile into the Mediterranean. He grew from this level of abandonment to the higher.

Picture 1 Here

Dara stood helplessly at the tip of the excavated ground at the back of their building. This was by the window side to their latrine. He was to pay his father the last respect. The perturbation of the faces around said much of his uncertain future. No more guardians for him. His mother left Papa when he could hardly recognize left from right. It was over twelve years now, and she never for once called to ask after his welfare. In like manner, Dara too has withdrawn his mind and to his memory, his mother was dead.

The populace only sympathized with the poor boy. No promise whatsoever was forth-coming to reassure him of a secured future from the sympathizers. They all have battalions back home to fend for. The native believed in polygamy. They also lacked family planning. Each woman in the home of a man with three wives might produce six children before a pause. Hence, they scarcely met the needs of their immediate family. This was to say Dara might be disappointed conceiving any of them for assistance.

Government and charitable formations within this populace lacked concerns for such responsibility except on the ground of show-biz or political inclination. People at the helm of such hierarchies were the sect whose inner disposition reflected the colour of their skin. Obviously, their level of sordid interest belied the commonwealth in their communal proclamation and cultural values.

Riro snuggled up to Dara as if she was going to pay hers respect too. Dara took the steps sideways to collect the shovel. He would be dropping the customary sand on the coffin of his deceased father. The young man again looked the side of the bitch, and he burst in tears. This was the only living being, next of kin or creature his father left him with. The only companion he would have to share their room and parlor with, lived with, ate with, talked to, and probably rubbed minds with. Riro, the only intimate friend and sister.

Dara bought this bitch when he was in class-one. It was from the money he had saved through his errand duties and casual jobs. Though the money could not make up for the charge on the puppy then but his father assisted him with the balance. Otherwise, he might not have been allowed to go with the puppy still after several days of delaying it for his sake. More so, his father assisted him to feed the puppy until it grew a mother-dog.

Riro's unusual scream about four days ago seemed to suggest to everyone that Papa might likely die on his sick bed. This consistent scream in the last three days to the incident was sufficient premonition to Papa's death. Papa finally left for the way of all the earth about the same period to confirm Riro's instinctive ability to nose this untoward end. Riro was moody thereafter, showing attitude of commiseration with Dara. Almost two days now, she ceased to eat. She went hunger-strike, deliberately refusing food. Dara was even afraid this might adversely affect her pregnancy. The sorrow was typical on her: her outlook was dull and sober; she apparently worn the earth on her skin. Riro wept alongside Dara earlier in the day. Both of them observed the proceedings, while Papa was eventually turned into the final carriage of all the living (coffin). Riro shed tears consecutively for a good while. She was very pale and down cast too. She knew the day was not a good kind for the household.

Riro loved Dara dearly because he normally took good care of her. Dara could afford to go hungry for Riro to eat. He rationed his food into equal part for Riro. He usually ate with her as if eating with a colleague. Whenever he swallowed a morsel, the next would be for Riro. Riro was a very perfect bitch who would not allow her portion of the food to hit the ground. She did this better when such food was a solid type. She grasped the throws from the space as soon as Dara released it. This cordial sharing could no longer make Dara ate in her absence. Dara kept the meal and patiently awaited her whenever Riro was not within reach at meal hour. Neighbors within the area believed their intimacy in this regard has its contribution on their likeness for each other. Twice and open, Riro displayed this likeness when a group of boys ganged up against Dara. They intended beating him up on that afternoon which was the second of its kind. Riro ran out of the corner of their parlour for his rescue having heard Dara screamed for help. On that fateful day, Riro would have bitten these boys if not for Dara who latter had to chase her away. This was because the dog had started growling and showing forth its fangs at these troublesome boys. Nevertheless she scrambled the boys in the dust before they could succeed to escape. Since then, everybody feared to fight Dara.

"If Riro catches you!" they usually said.

The little boy did as tradition required of him. He feebly held the shovel and threw the customary sand consecutively on Papa's coffin:

"Ashes for ashes."

"Sand for sand."

"Dust for dust." People chanted in accompaniment at each scanty drop. Hither, Dara could see Papa off.

CHAPTER 2

This was the summer of his fifteenth birthday. Dara has to struggle hard if he must live his dreams. Perchance, he has no better alternatives than to manage his life with the beggary wages from the menial chores and errand duties. He sat for his Junior Secondary School Certificate Examination lately. Though the result of the exam was still being patiently awaited. However, Riro would have to deliver her pregnancy and nurse the babies matured enough for disposal, if Dara would have to rejoin his mate in school. The school fee at the beginning of the new session was not negotiable. Hence, Riro's reproductive ability seemed to be Dara's only hope of accomplishing his educational quest. Otherwise, his aspiration to progress into the senior level of his secondary education might be truncated on financial ground.

This particular holiday season was the longest. It was the end of the year break and the holiday before another school session. The tallying of Christmas festivity at this period was also as good as an icing on the cake. Every bit of the travelling and new demands for playing kits soothed the holidaying children.

Christmas was finally here. Only few days separated the grand occasion. Children both of lesser age and of Dara's age who at this time have not yet gotten their Christmas attires disturbed parents seriously on this. The parents concerned too were not at rest to please their children. People flocked markets to get the possible best for their families. The More marketers inflated the prices of goods. Yet people trooped in and out of markets like swarms of insects. As if they have just been released from their confinement. Like the school children at the closing hour in schools. The gates leading to marketplaces have no definite closing time again. People narrowly have their ways through despite the wideness of such gates. Not only at the main gates, legs flooded all outlets to shops daily. People have to go slowly. Those who face this direction would have to wait for those at the opposite side. Just the way road vehicles got dispatched in batches to allow for free flow of traffic. The proverbial saying that "trekkers' know no hold up" was disputed in this regard. Goods were no more at a poor man's reach. Transport fare became darer. Only those who have their legs firmed on the ground financially could go for beef and chickens. Everything was exorbitant. Nevertheless people drained their wallets to get the possible things home for their families. They have to make their children happy.

Dara has nobody to turn to. Nobody to care for his needs. No parent to adjure for his own Christmas clothing like others. Anyway, this was not the first time he would be suffering such denials and emotional constraint. Dara never knew what it felt to be loved and cared for. Neither his own blood nor other fellow human ever accorded him a touch of care. Hence, he focused his attention on the Almighty God who could satisfy man's needs, asides his concerns for the bitch. A church-brother has taught him many things about developing a relationship with God. He taught him to pray our Lord's Prayer whenever he felt lonely and deprived thus:

"Our father who art in heaven,

Hallowed be thy name.

Thy Kingdom Come,

Thy will be done,

On earth as it is in heaven.

Give us this day our daily bread;

And forgive us our debts,

As we also have forgiven our debtors;

And lead us not into temptation,

But deliver us from evil…"

(Extract from the Holy Bible)

Even before Papa died, Dara said this prayer solemnly every morning, believing God for survival. Though the suffering persisted but the little boy strongly believed that better days could still be hoped for. He trusted God to see him through his education. At least, secondary school levels. However, unlike other kids of Dara's age who enjoyed love and protection, Dara was exposed so early to the mirror of life. He did face it squarely too, struggling hard each day to meet up with his challenges. The little boy battled hard to walk afar off the lane of emptiness that his ancestors plied all their lives. He desired the future in expectation of something more better. He detested to end up with the mere birth and death certificates like his predecessors achieved for passing the earth. Dara looked forward to a result oriented tomorrow. This passion kept him going.

Before his destitution could ensue petty jealousy of his playmate who oppressed him with their flamboyant attires, Dara withdrew indoors quietly to suppress his feelings. He said his prayers again and gradually came over the emotional torture. He started playing with Riro who has been very useful in this regard. she kept his company. Dara's paramount interest centred on how to secure petty jobs. He never enjoyed seeing the household going hungry. The little little money from the menial job has been sustaining the family. His colleagues who sometimes joined him to do such petty jobs now smiled to markets, having broken their safes. Some used the money to improve their wardrobes. Others bought toys and flashing things to stir their mate to jealous. Dara however remained spectator to the fun-fuss. Although the playthings were bewitching but he dared not used his money to purchase such things lest he suffered hunger with Riro. Dara passionately disliked seeing Riro yawning in hunger. Hence, he kept his money for feeding. Even if he would chase neither shoe nor clothing now, the challenge concerning nourishing feeding within this Christmas period remained his trouble. Going by the nature of inflation within the locality at this period, he might obviously be handicapped purchasing some key food ingredients. After Dara's estimation of all his reserve, it was glaring the money could not give him a good pot of soup. There was no provision for meat. Though he was able to secure a measure of grain (Rice). This would substitute the cassava-extracts they have centered their feeding on in the past many days. Dara strived hard but all his effort to procure meat for the soup did not pay off. It seemed they were fated to have soup without meat on Christmas. Hence, Dara felt so bad. He was not happy with himself on that Christmas Eve. He got angry at anything quickly, with anybody spontaneously. The night was approaching, yet, that apathy did not permit Dara to go prepare the stew contentedly. He sat on the pavement at the front of their house, frowning. Looking angrily as he watched his colleagues strutting around with their bangers and flashes.

Riro knew all was not well with her house mate. Although she did not know what exactly went wrong. She would have loved to inquire anyway, if only God could grant her such favour to speak like the donkey of Balaam (In the Holy Bible). But she kept her cool rather. She knew she must not make any playful advances to Dara at this point in time.

Picture 2 Here

Riro walked down to the middle of the narrow pedestrian walk way at the front of their house. An uncompleted building was facing theirs. Beside the building, there was a fence of bushes. It was getting dark, Dara maintained his position on their frontage. Riro stretched her forelimbs forward. She rested on the remaining two limbs behind, beaming his eyes in the illuminating darkness.

Obviously, it was about quarter after nine (9:15pm) that evening. There was darkness over the place. Electricity ceased to supply illumination in the environment as a result of the heavy rain that took over the atmosphere earlier in the day. The moon's refusal to smile on the firmament like the previous days also worsened the power outage situation. All of a sudden, Dara perceived certain violent movement. Thereafter, he began to hear strange noisy struggle between Riro and something yet unknown.

"Riro! Riro! Riro!" Dara persistently screamed. He could only hear Riro's acute growling as a result of the struggle. The boy could faintly see Riro from the distance.

Unlike the usual response, Riro despised this call and headed on, running fast after a thing. The struggle between Riro and this 'thing' persisted. Dara was troubled, Riro's obstinacy arose his curiosity. He needed to know what has engaged the dog in a duel. But just like the jovial comparison between mosquitoes and small children, once they stop making noise, you know they are into something. Thus, the sudden cease of this riotous struggle between Riro and the 'thing' rather further stirred Dara's curiosity. Dara quickly climbed down their pavement as a result. He has to look after Riro's welfare. At this time however, Riro has settled down. She turned back now to allow Dara saw for himself. She was wagging her tail as a sign of good tidings. Dara went for their lantern quickly. He reached the spot to discover it was a rabbit. Riro has killed a very big bush-meat to meet beyond their pressing need. Dara was over joyous. The Christmas soup would no longer be a dry one. He caressed Riro pleasantly. "Thank you, thank you," he said into the dog's ears, with a beam of pleasure in his voice. He finished the rest of the activities in the kitchen to make the soup ready for the great day.

CHAPTER 3

Brother Okonkwo was the fellowship leader. He came around often to invite Dara and his colleagues for the fellowship. Laso especially, Dara's kith and kin.

The boys were at Dara's frontage. They were playing table-soccer with bottle caps. Dara was very good at this game. He beat his colleagues one after the other. Sometime ago they made a trophy of iron, which was presented to the winner of that edition of the competition. Dara was trying to win this cup again. He had won it the first time it was presented. "Contest cup" they tagged it. His colleagues had contributed the sum of Two hundred and fifty naira {N250} to collect the cup back from him in agreement. Now they were placing the cup for the second time with an increase in the money that would be given the winner of it. Five hundred naira {N500} flat before the winner would have to release the cup. They have gotten a philanthropist now unlike before. The copper engineer whose official residence was a stone throw to Dara's building gave the cash backing for the competition. He loved watching this game whenever the children were playing it. Hence he was challenged to raise the fund for the competition. He also promised more gifts for the first, second and third persons in the ongoing table-soccer competition. Of course, he positioned his chair well at a distance accurate enough to view the game as the referee.

Mr. Mali knew these children could resort to violence if issues bothering on fair play were not properly resolved; since the competition involved financial rewards. Unlike the time past when the competition was for the fun of it. Therefore, he chose to be the referee to the game's proceedings. This gave him the free hand to decide against foul plays. He also gave the final rulings on argumentative issues. His decisions over ruled possible argy-bargy.

On such Sunday evenings, he freed himself of other commitments. No other occasion shared this moment. He wholly devoted it to thing-competition. Friends and associates who called to see him were normally directed to meet with him at the venue. This was where he has chosen to devote this leisure time of his. Reigning amidst the children as if he was still one. His wife has to succumb to understanding, so she was no longer disturbed seeing her husband as king amidst the children. She knew he could quarrel anybody who tried to obstruct him being free with children. He loved to share in their games. Aware of this, his friends would rather join him on their pavement-pitch. They kept whatever negative opinion about his action to themselves. Often, they got disturbed seeing him more committed to the game than the children. Hence, they discussed their affairs and went their ways. More so, when they discovered he gave more attention to the children's business than theirs.

Dara's team remained the defending champion. 'Lotto boys' was the name he gave to them. Each member of the team has own name as well. There was a robber-cap of certain tablet-container among them. He picked this container cap somewhere around a pharmaceutical store in their area. It was the captain to the team. Dara named it 'Pellet' for its flatness and right footed. There were three big ones too. These ones kept the back as defenders. They were pomade-container-caps. He called these ones 'The biguns.' Another renowned player was 'Marado'; it was the scorer. It scored the highest goals in the previous competition. Though there were no prizes for such players who performed remarkably in that previous competition. Such situation would not repeat itself in the current competition. There were tokens to be given for that type of outstanding performances. Hence, Dara set his things in order. He played them skillfully. Nevertheless Victor remained his fears. He had encountered Victor in the final of the last competition, and it was tough. Victor had almost defeated him. He was only lucky to secure a foul against one of Victor's thing-defenders. This foul gave Dara a penalty kick. This was the penalty his 'Marado' scored to equalize the lone goal against them. The equalizer led both teams into an extra time of five minutes each side. The extra time did not separate these two sides either. This brought about penalty shoot-outs. Dara's team got the upper hand in the penalties by three goals to two (3 - 2). Victor's selected thing-players had lost two penalties while Dara's team lost one to bear the lead.

Dara's skills in some other games other than thing-soccer was not doubtful. In fact, he was once a member of their community's juvenile football and track and field team. However, such credentials were not sufficient to establish him as the best in table soccer game. As far as that game is concern, he reserved the kudos for Victor. Victor played table-soccer with ease. His name might not be pronounced like that of Dara in other games but, as for thing soccer, he knew the in and out of it. He has good thing-players just like Dara. He also beat everyone who faced him played this game. Dara was no difference. Victor has not just started thrashing Dara in table-soccer. Record was available to affirm he was better off. Only that he was unlucky in the last competition, where he lost to Dara on penalties. Everyone, including the on lookers and their colleagues also knew it was by chance Dara thrashed him to lift the trophy.

CHAPTER 4

This was another competition. Dara's 'Lotto boys' in (Group A) was doing quite well. He retained his pride as the defending champion. He won his first two matches on good records of two-nil (2 - 0) against the first team he encountered. The second team also fell by four-one (4 - 1) within the normal thirty minutes set by the watch. He has two more matches before the quarterfinal. Victor as well, on the other side (Group B) was doing quite well. The group also contained five teams like the first. Victor was just scraping the heads of the opposing teams as he approached. He thrashed the first two teams in his initial derby. The third team he engaged at present has conceded three goals within the first fifteen minutes. In fact, there were predictions that the team would not concede less than six goals.

Dara watched the match keenly to study how Victor played it. He knew Victor might not know the better of other games but as for thing-soccer, he could play it anywhere: in school, at home, he was always Champions. Even if his parents should send him on an urgent errand and Victor saw people playing thing-soccer, he would stop and play a little. In fact, this least described how crazy he got about the game. To crown it all, Victor has good thing-players, and he was very proud of them all.

Although Dara has no match for the day but he kept watching to grasp the latest techniques as Victor displayed them. According to the draw, Dara might soon have his hands full against Victor. If he should scale through his preliminaries and quarterfinal matches, he would have Victor to confront at the semi-final of the competition this time around. Hence, he snorted when Victor advanced the goals against the 'Bridge boys' to five-nil at the tenth minute of the second half.

Bro. Okonkwo came around the neighborhood to look for Dara. The poor boy was somewhere amidst the thing-soccer-fans. Finally, he saw him behind the wooden pillar that held the extension of the building's roof. The roof shaded the pavement from the ray of the sun. This retained some comfort for the household during hot weather. The same informed the choice of this pitch for their thing-soccer matches.

"Hello! Dara,' brother Okonkwo called, 'how are you?"

Dara looked sharply behind to trace the voice to the presumable caller.

"Oh! Bro. Okonkwo, it's you. Thanks sir, I'm fine." He returned the greetings and saluted the fellowship leader respectfully.

He realized it was some minutes before five O' clock by his watch. He must have to leave for the fellowship immediate. This exactly brother Okonkwo came to remind him. Thank God the match which stole everybody's attention has just been brought to a close. He intended rushing indoors at once to pick his Bible before brother Okonkwo stopped him, asking questions.

"What about your friend?' He inquired.

"See him sitting over there." Dara made a gesture. He pointed in the direction of one of the windows to the uncompleted building at the opposite direction.

When Laso saw brother Okonkwo approaching his direction, he disappeared amidst the rooms of the uncompleted building within a twinkle of an eye. He knew brother Okonkwo would have nothing else to discuss other than inviting him to the fellowship. For this reason, he disliked brother Okonkwo. He felt bad that the man interrupted their playtime with his preaching and fellowship-member seeking. If not for Dara who usually gave him attention whenever he came around, he could have conspired with the rest of his colleagues to frustrate him coming. Sometimes, brother Okonkwo jammed Laso at the middle of the corner that led to Dara's house, but on those occasions the boy told him lies to escape. He promised vainly that he would come with Dara to the fellowship the next meeting at each of these encounters.

Brother Okonkwo lifted his eyes to discover Laso had dismissed himself from the window-frame upon which he previously sat. He advanced his paces into the inner rooms of the uncompleted building to see if the boy was dodging in one of the rooms. When he glanced the direction of the back door in his struggle to find him, he saw Laso Climbing the outer fence of the building for escape. In short, brother Okonkwo was marveled. Still in the confusion of the boy's reaction, he burst into laughter. To him, it was a surprise the boy's opinion of him was that bad. He wondered why Laso should be running away because he would be invited to Church. This was not a thing of force. Bro. Okonkwo also wanted to believe as well that it ought to be an avenue for spiritual growth. Only that Laso lacked this right attitude, otherwise, he would have have to help his education and parents in prayers by chosen to come for the fellowship. Besides, his visitation was never only about asking the boys to come with him to the fellowship. Dara alone explored other advantages of being the fellowship member amidst his colleagues .Brother Okonkwo normally sacrificed time to organize extra-moral classes for his student members. He coached them every Friday and Saturday evenings. This was his contribution to their improvement in their various studies. Despite their waywardness anyway, brother Okonkwo has made effort to invite Laso and his colleagues to these classes more than once. It would still have been of great benefit to them too. Yet, they turned down the offer and proved his effort futile.

CHAPTER 5

Dara emerged from their building. He obviously has over stayed indoors. He misplaced his writing Pad. He then must have kept bro. Okonkwo unduly waiting. This took him time to locate. But the fellowship leader's anxiety has nothing to do with his delay. Bro. Okonkwo looked frustrated. Laso's action was entirely responsible.

"Sorry sir,'Dara said quickly 'shall we proceed now?"

Hun!' brother Okonkwo snorted, smiling quietly as they proceeded.

Dara was happy for this freedom of his now. Gone were the days Papa would stop him going to Church. Papa would say he had better things to do for him than going to Church. Though Papa did pray, he normally said his prayers every blessed morning. Once he started such prayers, it usually lasted longer than necessary. Papa lingered on prayers. It attracted undue concerns most of the time before he would eventually bring such prayers to a close. Dara would have over stayed his time in their parlour, waiting for him to round such prayers up. Especially while waiting on him to collect his feeding money so he could leave for school. But Papa would not summarize these prayers. At times, Dara would be forced to create noise with table. He might also have to venture into dragging chairs in their parlour to interrupt Papa's prayers. Often, he shuffled his feet along the floor of their parlour incessantly before Papa would react and eventually stopped the prayers.

If not for these purposeful disturbances of his, Papa might continue such prayers for hours unending. He had chosen to be a prayer warrior in his bedroom. Only God knew what he prayed about. He would not care an iota for the little boy who loved to leave for school early to avoid being punished for lateness.

In spite of these lengthy prayers, it would be very difficult to convince an outsider that Papa was not a church-person. Although, he was a Christian by birth, but he hardly attended a church-service in his lifetime. Sometime, some church-people came to preach to him. Though they did not intend to bring him to church. It was only to share moment with him studying the Bible. Suddenly, they discovered Papa was no longer available to discuss the scriptures with. Today he would say a thing as an excuse, tomorrow another. On and on like that, until he finally instructed Dara to tell them he was not around whenever they called at his place. The poor boy had no option. He acted accordingly since he could not bite the finger that fed him. After several failed efforts, the evangelists also ceased coming. Papa had his opinion of churches. As far as he was concerned, churches were like any of these money making institutions.

"Their pastors are business men." That remained his stand whenever he heard people discussing Churches. He believed he was wiser than those church pastors who in his opinion cajoled people to donate money. In fact, it pissed him off whenever he heard his neighbors saying they gave to God, having donated money in Church.

"For how long shall we be deceived? Don't you all know where such contributions end? You know i will never be a party to such mediocrity. Pastors are getting fat at the detriment of the ordinary Church members. Those contributions week in, week out end up in their pockets. Or would they transfer the money to God in heaven? My pain in this matter is the collection of such fund in the name of God." That was Papa's argument with the last set of evangelists that visited him before he took ill.

Through out his life, his verba admission that he was a Christian had always been faulted by others. He did, particularly, editing duties on Sundays while others must have left for their place of worship.

Papa was the secretary to the chairman in their office. The nature of his job kept him in the office every other day of the week except Sunday. Sunday mornings therefore made good opportunity for Papa to edit minutes of the meetings previously held in their office. Muslims within the neighborhood had always believed he was one like them. In fact, Dara had had to argue constantly on his behalf that he was not a Muslim.

The journey to the venue of the fellowship was a short one from Dara's house. The service has commenced in earnest. They were making progress into another section of the meeting. After the opening praise and worship; iIt was Dara's turn to exult others in the word of God. The topic for this exultation has not changed: "How to observe our quiet time." This talk has been on rotation. It was an avenue designed by brother Okonkwo to build up the floor-members of the fellowship. Although, members would still get to listen to his message when it was time for the main teaching of the day. But for this meeting as it were, it has to be Dara first.

Actually Dara has not relented effort observing his quiet time as instructed by the fellowship leader. Importantly also, whenever he read a portion in the scripture, which required more clarification, he approached Brother Okonkwo. Brother Okonkwo has made it a point of duty too, encouraging bible discussions with him. He normally threw questions to Dara in the long run. At other times, he did ask Dara to quote and explain portions of the Scripture he read during his quiet time over the days. Dara has always proven to be a good student however. Hence, he could quote portions of the scripture off hand as a result of this exercise. Crowd-phobia however influenced Dara's speech in the course of the message he rendered at the meeting. Though he did excel other fellowship members who had spoken on the same topic during previous meetings.

The fellowship was soon over. Members were however mandated to pay one of the sisters a visit. She was marking her birthday. A get-together party was organized by the fellowship leader to celebrate this sister.

It was late before Dara could excuse himself from the birthday party. Riro yarned in patience for his return. In fact, she has at this time stationed herself at the front of their building. She declined the urge to stay indoors and looked forward in desperation to receive her house mate. It was unusual of Dara to stay out late, that she knew. More also, Riro was aware the boy must have gone to that usual meeting of Sunday-evenings. But she could no longer conceive his refusal to return when it was getting dark. Unlike previous sundays when Dara would have returned from such meeting by this time, this evening was different. The boy was not forth coming before the descent of darkness. Riro was very troubled: 'what could have hindered this boy's return?" She kept ruminating. The firmament yieldingly embraced the more of darkness. Riro's tension gained similar magnitude. She felt unease and dotted about. Although, the dog was yet to have her supper but hunger was not her problem now. Her concern was for this little boy whose return was not in sight at this unhealthy hour of the day. If something evil has befallen him, whom would she tell? Who would also care to join her search for him if the need arose?

Riro, hence, sat on her haunches at a corner of the pedestrian walk way by their frontage. Those who chose to follow this route that night were rather unfortunate. They ran into Riro at the extreme end of the channel. Most of these passers-by ran back to join other route. They thought Riro was there on purpose to waylay and pursue people. This was far from the dog's intentions. She sat in fever of impatience, looking forward to receive Dara. Though the day was readily entrenched in the prime of darkness but that would not debar Riro scenting out

Dara from a distance or amidst hundreds of people. She projected her head through the upright of her forelimbs which angled his shoulders. The hind legs balanced up the haunches on the ground immovably for minutes with anxiety.

What Riro has long awaited, Dara suddenly emerged. He took to singing as he plied the pedestrian walk way, approaching the side of Riro. The Dog jacked up elatedly. Her reaction was more of reflex. Her ears stood straight on her head promptly. She could not curtail her wagging tail from the excitement. Dara's return reverted her misery.

"Inhun! Inhun! Inhun!" Riro screamed in excitement, strolling back and forth in gallops. The dog was however known for this usual ovation whenever Dara returned from journeys.

In spite of the brewing agitation, Dara was yet to be aware of the dog's acrobatic parade in his honour. Perchance, it was due to the blackout situation in the environment. More also, the duo were not yet at close range. Dara would not have however claimed to be ignorant of Riro's 'inhun, inhhun, inhun,' rhythmic kind of ovation, but for a song he was singing. He learnt a new song at the fellowship. He has since been engrossed in the song, ranting:

"I must grow in all my day to day

In every department

Endeavors of my life.

I must grow in all my day to day

In every department

I shall not remain same."

Riro joined him immediately on his way, climbing up and down his knees in excitement.

"Wow! Riro, I'm sorry,' Dara said regretfully. 'I would have told Laso to help me with your food. Oh! I ought to have informed him earlier in the day, in case I arrive this late. It was an over sight, sorry."

Dara only grumbled on his negligence and delay of Riro's supper. Meanwhile, the dog was hardly bothered by the delayed meal. She was rather bugged by the young man's safety. Since no one was able to convince her all was still well with the poor boy.

The boy caressed Riro's head softly to appeal the dog for keeping her hungry. Dara knew she would not have even cooperated with the feeding arrangement through Laso. Though such arrangement, if earlier ensured, would have just been to extricate Dara from the quilt and possible blame of being responsible for her delayed supper. The dog was so fastidious about who provided her meal that Dara hardly bothered others to assist him feeding her.

Riro followed Dara indoors delightfully. The boy unlike Riro has filled up his belly at the birthday get-together-party. He lit the stove quickly to prepare some flour for Riro to eat.

{ **CHAPTER 6** }

Solo came calling, ranting Dara as he approached the entrance to their house. He has come to invite Dara for practice. He organized a football-club and being the coordinator, he used his school-fees to finance it. He purchased a leather ball and the jerseys. Solo was one of such wayward children who took their education for granted at the detriment of their future. His Dad was a retired headmaster. He was a very strict old man on matters relating discipline. Children who lived within his neighborhood could describe him better on this basis. They endowed him with unreserved reverence. The respect they could not accord their parents at home was reserved for him.

As an old man of about seventy, he has principles. If you must greet him, your jaw must touch the ground while prostrating. You could not choose to avoid greeting him either. Whenever a child greeted him and fell short of this standard, Solo's Dad would verbally combat the child, raking in his usual grammar:

"You're confounded! You this cantankerous child" If the child did not know what to do still; maybe he kept steering at the old man in confusion.

"Is that how you greet your father at home?" He would say to further accost him. 'Don't you know your jaw must touch the ground greeting an elderly person?"

A wise child would have been enlightened on what was expected of him by this last statement. If the child now adjusted himself quickly to do his bidding: "Oh! God bless you my son.' Mr. Akin would say in delight. 'Yes! There you're, you are greeting me now. Where did you keep that before? Your beard like that of the squirrel." He would then dismiss the child or attend to him after the gushing compliments.

Parents in that neighborhood did scare their children by laying emphasis on reporting them to Mr. Akin. This was common with mothers, since they were at the receiving end of this children's act of indiscipline. Mere mentioning they would be reported usually put these children in check. They succumb to obedience instantly. Only God knew why they were afraid of the old man this much. Some of these parents actually tended to believe it was because the old man was formerly the headmaster of the prominent primary school in the locality. That teacher's honor could not be toyed with. In like manner Mr. Akin has torture pattern for children who fell his victims. If he should flog a child, that child would not enjoy his trunk for the rest of that day as old as he was. He usually mentioned the number of strokes he was going to dish out before he flogged.

'I will give you six!' that was Mr. Akin's highest number of lashes. Further action of his would be to make the child serve punishment. If he however said he was going to flog, it scared his victims greatly. A lash of his was as hot as pepper. The option like it, if he said he was going to torture the child by dictating punishment, that would be an easy calamity for the culprits. Only to stool-down before Mr. Akin was normally on timing. The child would beg tears before the set time. Nothing interrupted such timing except he chose to change his mind. Such changing of mind however happened but in rare cases. Once he fixed the time the fellow languished in pains until the period elapsed.

There was a day a boy dared Mr. Akin. He spat up and told Mr. Akin to his face he could do him nothing. The old man quickly ordered the big-boys around to bundle this unfortunate boy into his sitting room. He dealt seriously with him. In fact, that served further as a deterrent to other notorious children within the neighborhood. Adeniji never again toyed with Mr. Akin's capabilities. In spite of all the fears and reverence however, Solo, the last child of Mr. Akin was the thorn in his flesh. Solo would rather run away than serving any punishment. If Mr. Akin punished the whole children in the neighborhood on an offence involving his son, Solo would be the only one to decline serving such punishment. Mr. Akin would not have deliberately left him unpunished but the boy repressed his reproofs. He out smarted possible moves by his father to punish him. His own stubbornness attained a level. This situation however nodded a proverbial saying right that 'If two Irons meet, one bends for the other.' Thus, Solo was no doubt a superior iron to that of Mr. Akin. At some points, Mr. Akin had resorted into using iron hand to counter this boy's idiosyncrasy, yet to no avail. At other times, he had embraced wisdom to handle him but it was the same result. Solo practically made his father incompetent in this regard. At present the old man would keep his cool whenever Solo faulted him. He would be waiting for the boy to come and sleep in the house so he could deal with him at the middle of the night. But Solo would rather run away from presumable areas near home. Mr. Akin would scarcely wait till around ten O' clock in the night. At this period the street guards would be preparing to come out on vigilante duties. He knew they could rough handle him. They could take him to be a watch-boy for thieves in the area, if apprehended at this period. Hence, Mr. Akin would have no choice than to carry lantern and began to look for Solo at every nook and corner of the streets within the neighborhood. The old man was just being careful not to allow the boy soiled the family name.

'Soloooo!' Mr. Akin would shout relentlessly. 'Come back home ooh! I will no longer beat you!"

Solo would emerge from a corner and returned the shout.

'No, I would not come! You will beat me."

Mr. Akin would quickly reassure him otherwise, begging him to come along to the house.

"I said I won't, I will not beat you again! God is my witness!"

Once Solo heard him sworn in the name of God, he would be rest assured he was not going to beat him. He then joined him to return home.

Elderly people, within the neighborhood who were eye-witnesses to this derogatory incident severally, said Solo's mother encouraged this delinquency in him. The mother was said to have over pampered him while he was much younger. She hid him under her bed to prevent his father flogging him whenever he did wrong. Ojuolape would rather tell Mr. Akin she had no knowledge of the boy's whereabouts after she must have hidden him. She encouraged this consistently until Solo grew wings. This was why Solo could no longer be tamed. He lacked regards for his father.

Solo ought to be in the senior secondary level of his education now, but somehow he was still in class two, junior class, because he was a truant. He played truancy lately with a whole academic year. At the end of the session, he stole a report card from the teacher's table. The dossier belonged to the best overall student in class two. Solo erased the name on it perfectly and, he carefully printed his on the relevant leaves.

When Solo got home with this report sheet, his mother was outrageously elated. She had had to party on this exceptional performance. She believed every record of the dossier about the inexplicable excellence of her son. Mr. Akin was doubtful of this in every form. Though he tried in vain to pick fault with the report because he could not see any traces of fraud on the dossier. The old teacher took his time severally to check the papers in and out. In fact, he ensured he had his magnifying glasses on before examining it, yet there was nothing fishy to query him about. Nevertheless, Mr. Akin knew the academic ability of this boy. This gave him the impetus to believe the boy had cut corners with this report card. He resolved within him to approach the school authority to clarify this.

Mrs. Akin was still knocking on doors within the neighborhood to spread the news of her son's exceptional performance when Solo's classmates came calling. The delegates came on the order of their class teacher to inquire into Solo's refusal to show up in school. Luckily, the class representatives met the boy right in their sitting room with the Dad.

At the end of the revealing drama, Solo fled, when the cat was eventually let out of the bag. He returned home three days after. His parents had it rough searching for him.

CHAPTER 7

The door to Dara's parlour was usually open. Once Dara noticed Riro indoors on his way out, he didn't bother again locking up. The house was usually in care of Riro until he returned. The boy was confident of Riro's ability to keep watch over the properties. She would never leave the premises in Dara's absence.

Riro would never harass Dara's callers especially when the boy was away, once such caller did not act funny in the bid to take things from the house. But once such a caller demonstrated such intentions, Riro didn't trivialize such attempt. She quickly began to growl at such fellow. In fact, she could resort into pursuing that person and showing her fangs in attack if he was a determined criminal.

This afternoon was a different case. Riro rose up from beneath the table. This was her hidden arena within the parlour. Solo was just few steps away from the door post. The dog was on his heels before he could make a reverse. She pursued him until the boy fell head over heels. Solo was roughened in the sand before the dog eventually withdrew. People within the neighborhood screamed out their surprises. They were mostly amazed because that was not the Riro they used to know. Not even strangers would have been as such molested by her. Neighbours within the surrounding who were eye-witnesses to this incident began to reflect on it in their own views. In fact, the dog's reaction that afternoon was a major issue on their discussion agenda for the day.

"Ha-ah!' if this dog will have to continue this way, Dara will have to dispose it." Babaijesha commented.

When the children around heard Babaijesha grumbling on this matter over again; '

Daddeeee!' they shouted.

This was a name Babaijesha would not tolerate anybody to call him. He just didn't appreciate it. But the children wouldn't hear him out. Hence, she began to rain curses on the children. He told them to measure him with their parents back home.

"He no go better for all of you who called me Daddy. Your parents will not gain over you! Yes! I will still report you all to your parents, and if they will not yield my complaint to tame you, I shall know what to do."

"Daddy! Daddy! Daddy!" the children's shout intensifying.

Babaijesha was so furious this time that he has to pick stones and began to chase the children. He was aiming to stone them.

"You said you'll not hear, okay," Babaijesha snorted, breathing restlessly. The children have made him run round the ring of buildings around.

"If you'll not hear,' he continued, ' by the time I break the heads of two among you with stones; you will hear."

Babaijesha was vulnerable to molestation because he was befuddled by impatience. He allowed children made sport of him unnecessarily. To him 'Daddy" the common name other men in their right senses cherished children calling them conveyed a different meaning to his hearing. It was abusive to him because he has no children. Going by his interpretation of this name as a Yoruba man, Daddy meant 'loneliness.' Daddy as literally pronounced, in Yoruba language meant "staying lonely." Therefore he would not take it light with anyone who called him the borrowed name.

Formerly, he fought people for calling him 'Tax collector.' He did not like paying tax, so he hated tax collectors. Tax collectors were however very much at work as at this period. They frequently blocked roads, stopping motorists and laying hold on passers-by {men} to confirm their tax status. During this checking exercise, Babaijesha would be constrained to stay indoors. He would not like to go anywhere until these activities ended.

The school children who noticed that Babaijesha usually hid for the tax collectors would rather expose him. Being impatience and void of understanding too, he yielded himself over to these kids who messed him up. He simply allowed these school children made game of him whenever they shouted: "Tax collector! Tax collectors are coming!" They scared him and fooled him about with this initially. Later on, this task collector approach lacked effect on him. Yet Babaijesha gave children another opportunity to molest him, the day it was discovered he would not like people to call him Daddy.

It all started out the day an innocent little girl from the city called Babaijesha Daddy. The girl had come with her mother to the remembrance ceremony of Babaijesha's great grandfather. Rahat was sent to pass a message across to Babaijesha. Innocently, she had called the old man Daddy, having no ulterior motive for doing so. This drama was at the frontage of Babaijesha's family house. This was the house Babaijesha inherited. The ceremonial activities were still very much alive at this period. The young girl was embarrassed. Babaijesha flared up and rebuked her strongly.

"'Why must you call me Daddy!" he retorted and fought her mother on this issue. He was asserting that her mother had sent her to insult him. Meanwhile the girl had only tried to be respectful, according him with similar measure of respect she accorded her father back home by calling him Daddy. To her, that should be the kind of honor one could accord an elderly man of his age. It was on the contrary rather when Babaijesha flared up, screaming to the world. This was the genesis of his predicament. He had personally uncovered his own flaw. This subsequently made a good chorus to get him unrest. The children would stop at nothing to find his trouble.

CHAPTER 8

D ara's return was somewhat earlier on this day. It wasn't that he was any good at brick work but the bricklayers enjoined him to come along always. Obviously, he was usually designated to carry block for the work men at such building site. He has had to interrupt the comfort of sleep as early as 5.00am on that day. Mr. Dauda had sent his son who informed him the previous night against their assignment at the market centre. The work involved decking and filling.

Everybody knew Dara was not a lazy boy. His hard working attitude encouraged the bricklayers sending for him whenever they secured new contracts. Not that carrying bricks was a thing of convenience for Dara, but he has to fortify himself against weariness to doing it. He was more afraid of hunger than tedious job. He detested the outcome of being lazy because, he could not help to watch their cooking pots embarked on compulsory holiday.

He was very happy that evening because the job paid off better than he envisaged. The workmen gave him two hundred naira {N200} cash after two meals. He returned singing his usual song as he approached their building. Dara was obviously very tired after the day's job but somehow, he could perceive this inner joy that propelled him singing. Such internal excitement naturally stirred him whenever something good was on his way.

Dara got home to discover Riro has delivered her pregnancy.

'Heeey! Thank God! Thank God!" Dara screamed his appreciation, expressing his feelings in delight. People within the neighborhood drew closer to confirm the basis for this excitement. As soon as Riro saw people coming around her again, she rose up to chase everybody. Then, it was dawn on them why the dog chased Solo earlier to stupor. Naturally, Dogs' temper was always on the high side during child rearing. Only God saved Babaijesha too this time. He left Ayo-olopon which he came around the neighborhood to play so he could poke nose into Riro's affairs. When Riro arose to chase, the nail holding the string to Dara's door hooked his 'agbada' behind.

'Yeh! Yeh! Yeh! help me!" Babaijesha screamed before Dara could come to his rescue. He helped him to remove the hem of his agbada from the doornail. Babaijesha then returned gently to continue his game.

Mr. Pappy had long awaited his return before Dara finally extricated him from the fury of Riro.

This was the sixth round; Mr. Pappy has thrashed Babaijesha five times. He employed the children's assistance to heap stones in front of Babaijesha. There were five stones already at his laps. This signified he has been beating five times. Though he did not enjoy the idea of setting stones before him in spite of his defeat. But, setting stones before the loser was one of the norms of the game. This eliminated argument on who won which. The winner of every round was declared without unnecessary inquisition.

When the current round also seemed to toe the way of the previous five, mockery ensued from the on-lookers of the game. Even, Mr. Pappy, Babaijesha's counterpart, did not help matters with his expensive jokes at the game's loser

'Nobody will deliver you from my hand today." Mr. Pappy emphasized. 'You will continue to fall like logs of wood in this game. In fact, the earlier you realise I'm your master, the better for you. It's therefore imperative you do whatever i bid you. Do you understand? Or else I thrash you again."

Continuously, Mr. Pappy made fun of his defeat bawdily. Babaijesha was silent. He could not say a word. Although, such jokes were absurd to him but he kept absorbing it. Probably, for the sake of the children around; he did not want to react foolishly this time. So, he strived at achieving some measure of dignity via self comportment.

When Mr. Pappy thrashed him again the sixth time, a storm of laughter broke forth. Babaijesha could no longer conceive it at this point in time.

'Wha! Wha! Wha! Wha!" the laughter continued for a period of time. It was a vibrant one.

"What's all this non-sense now.' Babaijesha retorted, with a display of higher magnitude of overwhelming anger. He rather directed his speech at Mr. Pappy. 'Mr. Pappy be warned o! Be warned o! I think I won't play this game with you any longer. Do you want to be dragging me in the mud before these ones? I think I will have to report you to Babaagba."

Babaagba was the owner of the Ayo-Olopon. Babaijesha has been playing this game with Babaagba for a longtime. Babaagba knew the in and out of the game over the years before others started learning it. So Babaijesha was at advantage to have grasped the techniques ahead of others. He has started playing the game long before others joined on. Yet, he lacked the capability to be the champion of the evolving generation at the game. Rather, a fast learner novice could end up taking him to the cleaner. His seldom defeat in the hands of Dara and other teenagers pointed to this fact.

No other Ayo-olopon user bothered Babaagba with issues of dispute except Babaijesha. Yet he ridiculously bawled about now and again with reporting threat.

What complicated issues for Babaijesha was the fact that he has no wife and no children. Whether or not he was impotent only God knew. But there was a story line that his kindred once wooed a woman for him in marriage. Although he was poor, because he was a lazy man who could not use his hands to fend for his living. He usually donated his blood to make a living. This was his only source of tangible income.

Babaijesha did not go to school; neither was he a craft-man. In his youthful days, he scuppered his chances to excel in life. He failed to do something worthwhile with his life in his hay days. Yet he loathed labor-job. This was why he suffered hunger often. He was shameless to beg people for money. Babaijesha could beg from a beggar. He asked Dara for money one day when the boy was returning from the market. He demanded twenty naira (N20) from the poor boy to eat. He still has not repented from doing this occasionally.

His kindred who took the wife for him had wanted to be responsible for her well-being. Only she should give them children through Babaijesha. They have much concern for him because he was the only male child of his parents. His sisters married wealthy men who enriched them also. Their intention was to perpetuate their family name through his descendants. But on a sunny afternoon, the woman packed out to come back never.

The story revealed that Babaijesha has strong passion for sex. He had almost torn the woman apart through sex. Morning, night and noon his chief business was sex. Of course, he has always been jobless. He has no other duties to preoccupy him. It was doubtful however if his semen could produce children. Hence, after few months of fruitless action, the woman took to her heel, lest he killed her.

As Babaijesha stood up in a rage against the teaming spectators who browbeat him in mockery, the children shouted again:

" Daddeeeee! Daddy Ilesha!"

Babaijesha did not like to be called Daddy talk less of being referred as Daddy-ilesha. Rather, he preferred his popular alias: Babaijesha. That pleased him than any other. By now, Babaijesha should be in his late fifties. Yet, he never behaved the age. He stooped quickly to carry the stool he was sitting on. He planned to hit the children with it, but they fled before he could make the move.

"'He no go better for your parents! Your fathers and your mothers would be the ones to Daddy, not me!" Babaijesha ranted, raining curses in response as the children kept shouting Daddy.

There was a day as such Babaijesha went downtown. He was surprised there were children within the area who knew him as Daddy.

"Daddy! Daddy! Daddy in the street!" the children shouted as they emerged in numbers from different angles on Babaijesha.

"Daddeeeee!" they all shouted on him in oneness. Furiously, Babaijesha picked stones and started chasing these children with it. But the children threw back stones at him in reaction. It was a rough game on this fateful afternoon between these two parties. When Babaijesha knew he could not prevail, he withdrew and started going his way.

Unfortunately enough, he felt like stooling when he walked down the street a little while. He couldn't suspend the nature. Consequently, he branched at the side of the bush nearby to excrete himself. The children at the other end knew he had stopped by somewhere down the street. They wanted to see to what he was doing at this busy end. They approached the spot to discover he had disappeared in the hedge of bushes. These children conspired to search him out with stones immediately. A fusillade of stone-shots threatened the environment. Babaijesha refused to voice out until a stone hit him on the head.

'Yeeeeeh!' He screamed his pains, 'your parents will not escape this ooh!' He touched the affected part and perceived blood. He rushed out of the bush immediately, fastening his trousers' rope wrongly.

"Help me ooh! The street-dwellers! Help o! They've broken my head. These wayward children!" He yelled continuously for help. The children had taken to their heels. People rushed out of their houses to ensure he was helped. Yet Babaijesha never learnt his lessons. He never ceased to exchange stones with children.

CHAPTER 9

Only Dara could touch Riro's puppies. Intruders dared not come near their parlor this time around. Riro lost the patience to entertain people around her puppies. Dara alone carried the pups every morning to play with and observed their gender. Dara was happier because the dog produced eight puppies at a time. More especially being her first attempt. She gave Dara three dogs and five bitches.

'That's good of you, Riro!" Dara appraised the dog's effort. He caressed her head in encouragement. Riro too wagged her tail pleasantly in acknowledgement.

Dara knew female-dogs would fetch him more money than male. He attempted a rough estimate of the whole amount he might likely realize at the end of the sales. He would definitely have a reasonable balance left over to purchase a pair of school-sandal, after he must have successfully paid the school-fee. This sensation refreshed Dara. His happiness knew no bound. He was happier because his schooling dream was yet alive. Dara however understood the need to fatten the puppies for the market.

He made a kennel for Riro at a corner in their parlour. The entrance door to the sitting room fenced the kennel to the wall. This corner was rooming enough to ease her nurse the puppies comfortably.

Dara didn't spare the clutch of eggs, which his fowls laid the previous weeks in ensuring Riro was well fed. He was burdened to prepare nourishing meals for her. This would definitely rub off on the pups. It would ensure their rapid development and healthiness. He also procured a smock of jelly fish. Beyond reasonable doubt, Riro experienced a change of feeding. In fact, bitches like her would love to do this again if this was what maternity could guarantee. Basically, her experience was history worthy.

Dara was rather happier the pups were born in good season. It was at such a sumptuous period while he has enough money to take good care of them. He worked hard over the past weeks to save an appreciable amount of money from the bricklaying site.

Gradually, the pups advanced in status. They soon began to move out of their harbor. They were tottering around the parlor. The exercise reassured their possibilities of gaining stronger limbs in matter of few days. This was an encouraging development. It buttressed the effect of the mother dog's good feeding. They have however begun to lay excrements over the places within the confinement of the sitting room. Dara would have resumed another disgusting duty packing excrements if not for Riro. The dog relieved him of this duty. She took care of the excreta with her tongue. This was simply because they have not started trying their mouth on farinaceous food. The juice content of the mother dog satisfied their feeding need at the moment. This was why Riro easily licked their excrement.

Nature soon encouraged the hand of time, the pups were weaned. Dara then began to prepare pap with raw eggs to feed the bouncing puppies. People who booked for them would soon come to take them away.

Rearing these pups from this point became the more burdensome to Dara. He prepared their pap, packed excrements and monitored their feeding every day before leaving for school. Riro no longer licked up the excrements. Besides, Dara would be confused whether to lock the puppies in the house, or free them to move around. Whichever decision, the two options have possible consequential effects. The pups would mess up the entire room if he should decide to lock them within the house. The alternative was more grievous, they could thieve them away if he should leave them unguarded into the environment. He was sure of this because everyone who saw them cherished them.

One day, Dara left for school forgetting the pups outside. Throughout the school hours he was not himself. A friend noticed his uneasiness. Though Dara tried to own up as if everything was well with him. Olagunju was quiet sure Dara wasn't himself. He drew closer after a while to inquire into what burdened his mind. Probably he could lighten his burden. If only Dara would be willing to share his mind.

"Dara' Olagunju tapped him from the rear, 'you look a bit prickly today!" What is the matter with you?" He inquired.

Olagunju was one of the fresh students in Dara's class. He abandoned science class for the commercial division of the Senior Secondary class when he discovered he might not be able to cope with the academic challenge of that class. He was wise to have taken such decision early in time before such switching became difficult. Anyway, Olagunju must have been a good observer amidst the rest of their classmates. Though, naturally, he seemed to get easily matey with people.

Dara was the class captain. He learnt some phonetic expressions from their lesson teacher, brother Okonkwo, who was a graduate of linguistics. He usually brought about something for the class to argue on in his incoherence grammatical composition. He stood constantly before the chalk-board to prove he was more versed in grammar. He did this whenever he has the instructions of their subject teachers to pass across certain information to the rest of the class. The fact that the students have not been tested by their subject teachers influenced this over dramatization of self worth by Dara and some other boys in the class. They were all products of different classes at the final level of their Junior Secondary School (JSS3). This was their first year in the senior class where there was a stint of specialization. Whichever field they have chosen here as SS1 students would, to a reasonable extent, inform what they might likely build on at the University level.

Dara was not comfortable discussing his problems with people. In fact, he did not believe in such things. He has always been all to himself. He kept the secret of his survival personal. He never went about begging assistant. Nobody knew how he ate and how he didn't. He restricted his survival to the world of his abilities.

Hence, the more Olagunju bothered him with more questions, the more he went dumb. He lacked explanation to the other boy's questions. Should he be telling him he was ruminating about the pups or what? Should he also begin to disclose to him he has been paid in advance on the same pups because of the need to settle his school-fee early? No, not on his life. He might never be able to disclose such to anyone. He hate when those who have things going for them favourably capitalized on that to molest other people with discouraging circumstances, especially in situation of quarrel. Dara obviously has a profound hatred for inferiority complex. He wouldn't allow anyone to put him in that shoe. This informed why he was always all to himself in situation of lack.

Hence, Olagunju was quite a victim of his concern because Dara's silence friendlessly probed him to know he was asking for too much. He continued entangling the hair on his head softly to deflect the boy's questions to the deaf side of his ears.

Olagunju looked him over again and again and finally left him. He retired to his table to mind personal business.

CHAPTER 10

Dara scarcely allowed the school janitor rang the closing bell twice before he fled out of the school gates. He ran tirelessly home. But to his amazement, Riro has shielded the pups on which he was troubled. She enticed them to a corner to suck. In fact, the puppies have since guzzled down on her breast. People could hardly notice they were at that corner. This was how Riro prevented them from scattering over the place. The following morning was a Saturday. This was the Saturday the owners of Riro's Pups would come and take them away. That was the agreement between them and Dara. These potential buyers were already within the neighbourhood for that single purpose. But it became necessary for them to exercise little patience for Dara to take Riro away from the environment. This would calm down the tension of having to wrestle Riro if they truly have to leave the surroundings with the dog's puppies.

Dara induced Riro with ball to their school-lawn. They usually visited this spot before now on Saturdays for practice. Though the whole essence of enticing her to this spot at this period was to forestall Riro's reaction against those who would pick the puppies. Laso attended to the puppies' buyers on Dara's behalf.

Riro did catch kicks whenever Dara played the ball to her. She used her limbs to stop such kicks. At times she pushed the ball back to Dara with her pointed mouth. Sometimes she danced around the ball as if she could dribble Dara with it. Riro liked this plaything so much that she normally got engrossed whenever she was allowed to participate.

Unlike the kick catching exercise, Dara and Riro were into field event this time around. Riro was running round the pitch with Dara. The boy was in training to accelerate his paces. He kept struggling on the lawn to outrun Riro. They started this exercise since the period Dara was on holiday. Riro's pregnancy hasn't become apparent at that time.

Dara was a strong representative in their school grouping, due to his performance during the previous Inter house-sports. He was a good athlete. Although, a boy named Fatai outran him in all the 100meters races at the junior cadre of the competition.

Fatai was presently one of the best athletes in the school. He wrestled his way into the position in his first year at the senior level. He has been consistent thereafter. Currently, he ranked among the four best athletes who competed for their school in inter schools' relay races and hundred metre dashes.

Fatai was a year ahead of Dara in school. While Dara was in class one (Junior Class), Fatai was in class two then. Dara came third overall in the junior category of the inter house competition at that time. Fatai came first while another boy in class three came second. Dara advanced the position the following year to come second when the other boy who was in class three graduated from the junior level to the senior category. Although, nothing was heard of him again in respect to athletics after his advancement into the Senior Level that year. Fatai who was then in class three maintained the lead in his usual first at the junior level. Another class three student, trailed behind Dara to pick the third position that season. Throughout his junior classes however, until Fatai left the junior category, Dara was not able to come first. Fatai joined the senior category cadre of the inter houses competition in his first year at the senior secondary level. The boy outran all his seniors. This was how he toed his way into the heart of the sports authority in the school.

Dara also longed after recognition. In fact, probing his intentions, he desired to outrun Fatai. Fatai was his sole obstacle attaining the first position in the junior years. He curiously looked forward to win a shirt amidst the four best athletes of the school too. No doubt, such aspirations required a large heart and of course, the young man's ability to take the bull by the horn. Though instinct informed him he could do it, but he really has to intensify his practices. Riro's availability would be a plus now that she was on baby break. Obviously, Dara knew he wouldn't have to negotiate improvement if he must be accomplished.

Another inter house-sport was approaching. St. Anglican Secondary School revealed a new look. Students have been preoccupied with weeding and general sanitation since the beginning of the session. They have to cut the grass to shape. They have to renew the field's tracks. Junior students brought pegs to cut a spherical circle at the middle of the field. The various students groups intensified training and constantly practice to keep their representatives in shape. Individual student too, who was going to bear the colour of their group took to personal training. Every participant expected a classic competition. They all looked forward to carry the day for their group. The entire students were grouped into four. They regarded the four groups as houses.

Dara re-structured his personal training program. He now ran several kilometres every morning with Riro. They usually got up by 5.00am every morning. They maintained the route that led to the side of the River downtown. After running several kilometres before getting to the shore of the river, they still maintained timing discipline while running side-ways at the plain of the river's shores. This was Dara's training routine for the period of the competition. Dara has obviously de-emphasised class attendance for this self-developed training programme of his in the main time. Although, he still managed to participate in few classes after observing enough relaxation at the end of his morning exercise. As soon as he was set for the school however, Riro ceased to accompany him about. He definitely has to leave the dog behind while leaving for school. Though Riro has always made attempt to follow him to school. At least if he was a partner in training, while not a companion to school. So, whenever Riro made the move to join him to school, Dara would shout at her to go back. There was a day as such Riro followed Dara to school. Her presence was serious distraction to both teachers and students alike. Everybody blamed him for bringing his dog to school. Since then, Dara never negotiated bringing Riro along within the school hours.

. This should be a reminder to the day Riro followed Dara to church on a Sabbath. The Church-Ushers resumed another special ushering duty on that day. They explored all known tactics to pursue Riro from the entrance of the Church to no avail. Obviously, Dara was ignorant of the dog's company on the way. Riro had trickily followed him at a distance behind. She did not move near Dara at all on the way. She knew the boy would chase her back if her company became knowledgeable to him. Hence, she arrived at the Church premises with Dara uninterruptedly. Her presence was a disturbance to the Ushers at every of her attempt to gain entrance into the Church while the service was alive. Probably she had in mind a special number to render to her maker like their choir. But the Ushers raised alarm. This brought Dara into the consciousness. He stepped in to pursue Riro from the vicinity.

Dara was still bent on this urge for glory. This ensured the continuity of the personal training program he has drawn up for himself. A day after another, he has had to run his heart out competing with Riro at the river side. The duo again furthered on their escapade and continued their daily marathon to the river bank. It was just a few minutes past Five o'clock that morning. Riro's company was the courage boaster that gave Dara all the confidence against the possible threat of the lonely hours. She served as his body guard. Otherwise, the inhumane calmness of the beach alone would have choked his desire for the early morning training.

Their normal activities soon came to a close on that fateful morning. Dara advanced his steps towards the far bank of the river to observe the condition of the fishes at that hour. It was just about the peep of the day. Thus, there was a dim brightness over the sky. Due to the heavy down pour over the night however, there seemed to be a calm silence in the environment. People in the neighborhood still struggled with such alluring breeze that enticed further sleep. So, individuals who usually fetched from the river at such early hour of the day were yet to be sighted. This buttressed the fact that the people have unconsciously negotiated preparation for the day's activities with the comfort of the hour.

Riro sat on the strand at a distance behind. She was still gasping for breath with her mouth wide open, having just retired from their normal races. She sat on her haunches, awaiting Dara to come and lead the way back home. Suddenly, Dara slipped from the moist plank at the river bank. He was just still trying to lift his right leg in his attempt to withdraw his look.

'S L A S H!" the water spattered from its barricaded area. The splash obviously spit on Riro where she sat. The Dog arose immediately. She knew something magical has happened. She looked curiously around for Dara as if he was dodging her. She however heard the little boy's scream. That was an indication Dara was in danger. Riro was at first hesitant. She was confused with action. Hence, she waited in fever of impatience if only the boy would resurface. The dog soon began to scream in her solemn manner: "In hun! In hun! In hun!" That was the appealing strains of the dog's cry.

She ran agitatively up and down as if looking for helping hands to rescue this boy. She knew that must be an unfortunate incident.

Why would the boy have opted for fish observation at the time they ought to be heading home?

Riro lifted her pointed nose up, ' In hun! In hun! In hun!" she screamed incessantly as if that could touch God to send help from above.

When neither man nor angel appeared as far as she could observe. Riro turned her back and ran up the steep bank of the river. Dara has been struggling for a way up too from the deep river obstructing him. He was not familiar with swimming. Only God knew the last time he took a bathe inside river.

The river was deep, reaching his neck. This implied, he would have to bury himself in the water if he has to advance. This was his problem. Dara could scarcely stay a second breathless in the river. Hence, he could not swim and was left floundering in the deep end of the river. The fence to the river was not his problem. In fact, such barricade lacked the height to cage him. But getting to the fence was his headache. Dara could not just bury his head to swim.

It wouldn't be a laughing matter however, should the inhabitants of this vicinity get to sight Dara in their river. They looked after the cleaningness of this river because they used it in their domestic activities. Consequently, they would not take it light sighting anybody bathing inside the river or urinating around the shore. In fact, they drank of it in dry seasons. This was why Dara needed to get himself out of this river quickly or else he would be in for it. He would definitely have himself to blame if the people should come and see him swimming in the river.

The day was getting brighter, all his efforts to make slide moves proved abortive. Riro jumped into the river at once. She moved quickly to Dara. Dara in turn held on to Riro as a support. The dog placed her head on the water surface, floating and heading towards the river's barricade. They arrived in a jiffy. Dara immediately stretched forth his hands and surmounted the barricade without wasting time.

Now Dara was safe but Riro was left winking in the river. In fact, she presently struggled to keep floating. Her strength diminished. The lad could not go home without her. The inhabitants must not see her in the river either. In fact, hers would be worst. Nobody would stop them not to kill her. Hence, confusion set in. Dara could not jump back into this horrible river. He could not leave for home without Riro either. He blamed himself for being impatient. Everybody would have been happy now if he did not hurriedly climb for safety instead of helping Riro up first.

Dara stood still, 'What manner of unlucky morning is this?' he ruminated. Riro was now catching cold in the water, very helpless. She kept steering at Dara on the other side of the fence. Dara longed for Riro passionately. His soul yearned as if he should jump back into the water when Riro started to scream: 'In hun! In hun! In hun!' Unfortunately, jumping back was as death sentence to Dara. He was already cold inside out. He knew he could be fated jumping back because there was no strength left in him. Consequently, Dara burst into tears in compassion for Riro.

When Riro saw Dara weeping and possibly helpless towards the situation, she turned her back for a show of courage. Since she was also an athlete whether in the open or at the corner of their house, she prepared her mind for the heighten jump. Besides, she usually jumped the small gate as a barricade to goats at their entrance back home. Hence, Riro looked round to discover the fence was lower at the bush end. She approached the side quickly. She jumped over the barricade with her reserved energy.

Dara was very happy to see Riro coming out at last. He rushed up to meet her immediate. He embraced her warmly as his token of appreciation for the gallantry.

CHAPTER 11

Despite Dara's strenuous practices, he remained a runner-up to Fatai throughout their friendly attempts in their house grouping. Dara became very discouraged. He was not pleased that Fatai would continue to stop him from achieving his aim. Though he lacked the answers to how better he could improve on his performance, having done all to no avail. Fatai was a hard nut which others never found to crack on the track and field event. Dara was not only his victim. He has deflated numerous other student's aspiration within and outside St. Anglican Secondary School. Dara eventually shore up himself to intensify practices against the school inter house sport. Perchance, he might still get some pride from a good race.

The school was decorated from the school gate to the extreme end in the damp. There were painted stones round the playground. Many administrative blocks have been repainted within the school. The lawn looked charming. Multi-colored balloons were used to adorn the canopy at the core of the field. This reserved arena accommodated the visiting dignitaries on the occasion. These V.I.Ps include: renowned men and women within the locality. Principals from other schools, representatives from PTA association and members of staff of St. Anglican Secondary School. The sitting arrangement was also in accordance to this listing order.

Many of these invited guests from the locality bore the names given the houses into which the students were grouped for purposes of the competition. It was yet another thrilling moment, jam-packed with events.

The program commenced solemnly with an opening prayer rendered by the principal of a neighboring school. The opening speech revealed the order of program. This was done by the moderator of events.

The march past parade came first, and the students marched out in groups. They wore vests signifying the colours of the competing groups. The vests also bore the name of each of these houses. The competing students were all in white sucks. They passed before the guests and the panel of judges in uniformity of movement. The panel of judges would decide the contest based on their marching parameters. Drums rolled in constant tones, dispatching the competing groups in their order of troops.

The program progressed on the order of the moderator. On-lookers were enjoying every bit of it. Now the four by 100 metres relay race has just ended. Falope, Dara's house came second with the help of Fatai who received the last baton to outrun two competitors. The boy who took their second lap had almost scuppered their chances before the baton got to Fatai. Fatai put up a wonderful performance for their house. Otherwise, they would have lost out completely in the relay race. Everybody ranted "Fatai! Fatai! Fatai!" When the boy overtook two of his counterpart on the relay tracks. Dara was partly jealous when Fatai won the on-lookers' praise. Though Dara started out the race. He took the first lap of the relay race and he did give his best too. It was the boy who took the baton from him that rubbished his efforts. The boy was really a disappointment to have arrived last before handing the baton over to the third person. The fact that the boy put up a wonderful performance during their preliminary practices prompted their housemaster to enlist his name for the race. Crowd phobia however crippled his ability to do well at the event proper.

The boys were already on their marks for the last 100-metre dash. Dara knew this was the last opportunity he has to prove his worth. May be, he needed to outrun Fatai to make a mark. They were the focus of all eyes. Everybody knew Fatai was going to carry the day again regardless the involvement of the final year students. Though these final year students possessed better body structure befitted of some sort of borderless-class athletes, but their beefiness might not make much difference. Fatai was always the champion unless he didn't participate in such race. Fatai has done it before. He could still do it. The bigger boys might not be able to stop him clinching his regular first position again on this remarkable day.

Dara's heart was beating rhythmically. Good athletes like him were still unknown to the school. He was as light as a bird-feather on his mark. They were all awaiting the take off whistle. If only Riro could come to his aid at this point to lend him the swift limbs.

Picture 3 Here

' P r o o o o h !'the die was cast and there went the whistle.

Dara was as swift as a rolling wheel. He took off nice. He was going briskly enough in his best. It was the competition of all the competitions of this great event so far. The most senior ones in their final year knew this was the only chance they have gotten to redeem their image. They have to find the way. One of them needed to regain the first position. So they were really stretching it out to stop the junior ones outrunning them, especially Fatai. Whereas, Dara decided for no other position than first. However, Fatai remained the swift gazelle of the school. The records have been constant over time. Hence, the competitors were really competing. The whole pitch was gravely. It was an interesting sight. People's eyes were keen on the athletes. A crucial moment indeed that arose several questions in the minds of the on lookers: would the most senior ones fail to check Fatai? Would Fatai do it again as he did to make the school proud in inter schools' competitions? Which of the competing houses would eventually win this race?

There was no question as whether a new star could emerge or not. This was because the existing stars were still unpleased with the neck bearing the first shirt amidst them. They would stop at nothing now to cause a change. Though the two previous competitions as test cases revealed Fatai was currently second to none in that school.

Dara alone was in class one in the midst of these giants. Although if Fatai came first, their house (Falope) would still carry the day. But importantly, people would be concerned with who made the name.

Now it remained just few paces to the verge of victory. Dara at the front line. His mind was readily in flame for honours. But somehow, all other athletes were behind him except Fatai. He was thinking he has done it at first until he saw Fatai at a pace beyond his. The boy could not just have been able to do it better than this. He could not have increased the velocity at which he was moving now. In fact, this should be his season's best. Thus, he gave in to fate that he might never be able to beat Fatai to it.

A few steps to the finishing line. The spectators were tensed curious in fever of impatience. Suddenly, Fatai fell at the verge of victory to allow Dara carried the day. A shindy arose from the astonished on-lookers. The ovation was quite laudable. Nobody expected it. Nobody could think into it. That a boy in class one would come first amidst the beefy guys? People took to the pitch as if it was a world cup victory.

Picture 4 Here

As if the entire program was all about the 100 metre boys' final. Dara was carried shoulder-high. Other students left the scene of events to chant his praise.

People showered gifts on Dara. He also received some reasonable amount of money on this lucky day. The on-lookers' concentration was wholly diverted. In fact, the rest of the proceedings no longer appealed to these teaming on-lookers who rather went after Dara in jubilation. It was obviously a history referencing success. Dara became the cynosure of the event. He was indeed too young to have put up such performance. This was live and open before the entire students, the panel of judges, their game master and the principal to the school. Hence, Dara as well registered his name among the notable students of the school.

The area-boys ensured he was shielded from attack. They securely took him home when the senior students initiated fracas on his case. Many of these senior ones were not pleased with this success of his. They considered it an embarrassment, especially to their representatives.

Hence, they were attempting to injure Dara before the street-boys came to his rescue. More so, they had attempted to plunder him of the gifts. It was a serious scuffle between the street-thugs and these hooligan-students before Dara could escape being molested at the school-gate.

Within a twinkle of an eye, everyone else was in jeopardy. These rivaling parties have turned the school gate into attack spot. The rowdiness hijacked the continuity of the program like presentation of gifts to befiting individuals and group. This was because the school lawn has eventually been overtaken by the rioters. These bad boys threw broken bottles and chairs into the field.

The participants and other students were in disarray. The teachers, the principals and other dignitaries who came to grace the occasion struggled to find a place to save their heads. Dara was trouble free. He was back in his house while his mate craved safety within the school arena. This credit actually went to the area boys who fenced him out of the premises. Their action in this respect obviously demonstrated the adage that "Notorious people have their days."

Students who bore grudges against their teachers seized this avenue to assail them. The rest of the staff have had to lock themselves up in the school's staff-rooms, appealing in supplications to God for safety.

The street-thugs went after these hooligan students with axes and machetes. It was terrible before the interventions of the police. Many rioters have lost one part of their body or the other. In fact, many were bayoneted to death.

Innocent students ran into the bush to save their heads. Friends have lost in touch. Everybody struggled for his or her own life.

Normal activities in nearby streets were interrupted. Marketers and passers-by ran helter-skelter. They rushed into available houses around to hide their heads. Women who have not yet seen their children agitated about and kept hollering their names.

The police shot tear-gas in the air to dim the eyes of the rioters. They took control of the situation afterwards and caught some of these people disturbing the public peace. Thirty minutes before then, two among the final year students who initiated the fight were reportedly confirmed dead. Some others were seriously injured. An unspecified number of the school's window blinds were vandalized.

One of the teachers during interrogation said he was given the beating of his life. In fact, the hooligan students deflated the tyres of his vehicle in his attempt to zoom off. 'Only God saved the windscreen.' He testified.

Broken bottles and chairs littered the playground. Without doubt, the incident adversely affected the good reputation of the school.

CHAPTER 12

This was Dara's second year at the senior level of his secondary education. He was in SS 2. Their promotion exams was approaching. It was not going to be business as usual. Only sound students, education wise, could make it to the final class in their school. Though Dara didn't have problem bending his mind to his studies. But he definitely has to double his effort this time around . It really affected his playtime with Riro. This was a duty call he wouldn't negotiate for anything. He could not jeopardize his future for playing around. Riro obviously succumbed to understanding. She reduced her playful advances towards Dara.

The fortune of war, they said, creates strange bed fellows. This was exactly what Dara's fame and prominence brought about. So many ladies in St. Anglican Secondary School now flocked around him in flirtatious manners. Some often made outrageous advances to attract his attention. In fact, the ones in his classroom would not give him a respite. This was not just because Dara was a brilliant student. His current status as the President of the just created social club in their school added its influence. He won the post through the procedure of election. Majority voted for him in the pool. This was an election conducted at the beginning of the session to vote such lucky students into positions.

Other contestants as Dara had campaigned round the school classrooms like politicians. They all tried to win the favor of other students. Apart from the post of the president, there were lesser positions. Other students also competed for these positions. The post of the president was however the toughest in the contest comparably. Other posts in contention include that of assistant president, secretary to the president, financial secretary and so on. No doubt, the presidential post was rivaled among renowned students of the school. Dara however stood tall amidst other competitors. The record he broke as an athlete was one of such pluses that gave him a hedge over others. More so, he has an alias which was as prominent as the school's name itself. The least student in their school recognized with him. Everybody called him Darosa. With this unbeatable reputation, he won the seat. "The Presido" of social club. Hence, St. Anglican secondary School no longer made complete pronouncement without infiltrating Dara's name. "One Saint, One hero" made a good slogan for the School within the locality.

One day, Sola, the most beautiful lady in Dara's class came around Dara in her usual disturbances. Kemi and Bose as well drew closer to interrupt his silence. They were making effort to get him play with them. Dara was however indifferent to their advances. He has since pre-occupied his mind with issues of survival relevance.

He has been very concern lately about raising his WAEC fee. He knew the time was almost very short within which the school authority allowed for students to raise such fund . Besides, he has no parents anywhere who could readily dispel his fears about the fee's challenge. These and more bothered Dara. Though Riro's pregnancy ensured some measure of confidence but he was afraid Riro's pups might not have weaned before the payment. Only if he could demand advance payment from those who would be interested at purchasing them. This young man was determined to attain excellence in his pursuit to change history. He strongly believed, it might take so long but the yellow-river would eventually kiss the sea. Dara never negotiated courage. He looked straight in the race towards achievement. The schooling project was the only bee in his bonnet for now. As far as he was concern, women matter was secondary. That could always wait until success kissed his effort.

Dara placed his hands on his locker. The locker was made of Iron. He stretched his legs behind the locker's poles. Sola stood right before him. She wanted him to respond to her playful advances. Dara was rather partially minded of her activities. She therefore dragged the locker in her struggle to gain Dara's attention.

"Yeeeeeh!' Dara screamed. The locker has inflicted pains on him. It pinned his toe to the floor with the manner at which Sola drew it. Consequently, it has flayed the cuticle of his toe-nail. It was obviously a deep cut. Deep enough to negate possible first aid attempt to stop the gush of blood.

'What's the matter with you?' the ladies jokingly demanded. They were never knowledgeable of the injury their unguided advances have caused him.

'It's no joke! You've wounded me!' Dara screamed in pains. He drew the leg forward quickly, blood streamed unstoppably from the cut. More so, it was a sunny afternoon. His blood was warm. Hence, Dara was rushed to the health center. The health workers eventually brought the blood under control after several minutes of battling with it.

The ladies were very sorry, having inflicted untold pains on him. Sola really regretted her action. She never envisaged it could be that bad. She came to Dara severally to say she was sorry. In fact, she practically abandoned her seat for Dara's table. The owner of the seat beside Dara had to excuse her so she could sit by him.

At break time, Sola bought him egg-pies and cold juice. She spread her pullover on him. Her caring touches soon influenced side attractions; as such that everybody began to call her Dara's wife. The lady was rather pleased with that. She seemed to have gotten an advantage over other ladies who desired to get closer to Dara now. In fact, other ladies appeared jealous. During their lessons in the afternoon period, she wrote his notes for him.

The incident badly influenced Dara's health because he lost much blood. He scarcely went to school. Even within the few days he made effort to, he felt ill at ease, battling dizziness during their lessons.

Sola now followed Dara carrying his school bag home. She assumed the duty since the day of the incident. In fact, she visited Dara's place every morning before coming to school. She assisted him with domestic chores before leaving there for school. This was in addition to the food flask she brought for Dara from home every morning. She also prepared Riro's meal in Dara's house. In fact, Riro was gradually getting use to her.

Riro nursed Dara's wound until the toe healed up. She dressed the wound every morning when Dara stretched the leg forward. She removed the mucus with her tongue and dressed it with her saliva. These nursing activities of the dog saved Dara some medical expenses. Riro was all there for him.

CHAPTER 13

Dara would be addressing the school assembly on social day. What an opportunity to have a voice. The young man would be held in honor before the entire students, the teachers and even the principal of the school. He was to deliver his paper as the president of the social club. Hence, Dara began to demonstrate it out first with Riro at home. He usually positioned Riro before him as if she was the audience. He would then take his stand at an arm's length talking to Riro from the paper he prepared for the address. As soon as he began to twist his accent to reflect that of the Americans, Riro would sit back like a spectator who understood every bit of the message. The dog has always proven itself to be a sensitive creature who got serious when Dara was. She overwhelmed him with play too whenever Dara called for such. This civilized Riro.

Dara was held in honor on their day; Social-Club day. He sat beside the principal on the high table. The platform was gorgeously decorated to reflect the glamour of the occasion. It must have cost an effort. Artistic touches were evident.

As the host of the occasion, he was honorably announced and invited to the microphone for his address. Dara in like manner stood to the microphone and rendered his speech fluently. The students applauded him again and again. Some made a rhythm of his alias, shouting: 'Darosaaaaaah!' 'Darosaaaaaah!'

Dara's fame traveled beyond the walls of their school.

The school examination time table was soon published. Rigor work commenced. Although, Dara has never relented his effort reading his books before then. But he needed to double up now. "To whom much is given, much is expected." He has to keep the fame intact in all facets.

Dara woke up as early as six every morning to prepare for school. He has reasons to be punctual. His appointment as the senior prefect pointed to this direction. It was just that he stayed up late lately, reading all through the night. Sometimes he read till 3.00am. Whenever he stayed this late however, Riro who was familiar with his school preparatory hour woke him up. The dog would begin to bark at this particular hour like an alarm clock set specifically at a time. Riro's activities would forcefully rob Dara the comfort of that hours when sleep sweet most. On and on like that until their exam period expired.

CHAPTER 14

Day by day, Riro lost her abdominal precinct to the elastic cervix of pregnancy. This was a sign of healthy growth in her advanced womb. The babies were really doing well on her inside. The holiday period was gradually winding up. Dara has begun to notice symptoms of delivery judging by the dog's natal status. Just the signs he observed when it was getting to the time Riro delivered the previous pregnancy. Dara has fathered his schooling plans on the proceeds from this pregnancy. He would be using the bulk part of the money to pay up his WAEC fee. He would also settle other petty bills, bothering on his school bursary. 'It depends on the number of the pups this time. If only she could increase the tallies. Presumably, by two, bringing forth ten puppies. Proceeds from such will definitely be sufficient to settle my bills. At least, with such an amount at hand, I'll also be empowered to stock the kitchen with nourishing provisions after the payments." Dara brain-stormed on this and swallowed gushes of saliva consistently as he ruminated.

Irony and illusion, often have they demonstrated they were no mere literature. Snail moves, erecting its antennal. Everything in life comes and goes in their course. In fact, no single day of a man is ever alike. Just like the wise saying which stipulates that man proposes but God disposes. Christened on a Friday about two years ago, but ironically, the same Friday occasioned her gory transition.

The same breeze that blew cool was to blow doom on this ill-starred day. Dara's unusual sense of burden and restiveness was an unnoticed incursion into the looming irreparable damage of this unlucky day. Dara dotted about and was practically uncomfortable right from the moment he stepped out of bed that morning.

The seer of Dara's house who fore saw Papa's death lacked the spiritual ability to nose this particular disaster also beforehand. The inability to such sensitivity therefore justified the saying that: 'he who knows his end knows his fortune-day" so claimed the adage.

The wind blew gently, it was not too hot but a serene noon hour. Obviously in variation to a few days before then, it was not a sunny afternoon. This was the type of afternoon the marketers, the hawkers and pilgrims would naturally adjure God for. Office workers were yet to return. This implied the day was still very young. School children were still on holiday. Though they have began to count down on the few days left for the holiday to lapse. These holidaying children however barricaded all the open streets within the neighbourhood, playing football. 'Monkey goes to market and never returns."

Riro suddenly left the neighbourhood and began to go towards the market place. Dara sat innocently on a chair at their frontage. Only God knew what business has Riro in the market place. She was with Dara a couple of minutes before this period, sharing some roasted corns with him. Dara was busied with a magazine immediately after that lunch.

When Riro got to the middle of the road at the market centre, a taxi emerged from where nobody could actually make sense of. It hit Dara's lover hard on the abdomen. She fell bleeding at the spot. The taxi driver escaped. Those who knew Riro with Dara have begun to groan in pity before his arrival.

The poor boy was soon struck by the news of this fulfilment ravaging tragedy. He ran willfully to the spot of the accident. He could hardly believe his eyes Riro has been knocked down by a taxi. He went down with the same speed at which he approached the spot to lift the dog from the pool of blood. The fear of blood-stain was not to him a consideration judging by the way he curdled the wounded dog.

Dara noticed she was still breathing in bits. Hence, he was pricked to rush her to the veterinary centre, probably they could rescue her life for his sake.

Dara hurriedly made effort to wave down vehicles heading the direction of the pet centre. More than three taxis have driven passed him now. No one cared to give him a lift with the bleeding-dog. Dara looked into Riro's face again to observe her condition. Tears influenced his cheeks.

' Riro, why did you do this to me?" He said softly into Riro's ears. The dying dog heard his compassionate voice and blinked her eyes in passionate response. Though in agony of death.

When Dara remembered the pregnancy, the water running his cheeks increased. Hence, he advanced his steps onto the middle of the road when another taxi emerged. The driver was forced to march his break immediately: 'O o o o o w!' it sounded. When the driver noticed Dara would not allow him the right of way, he alighted. Dara drew closer in tears, appealing the man for a lift. The taxi driver eventually considered his plea. He parried the bleeding dog with his laps to prevent blood-stain on the public seat of the hackney carriage, mowing supplications until they arrived at the pet centre.

The veterinarians did their best to bring Riro back to life. If not for anything, they could have done it for Dara's sake. He prayed them in tears not to allow Riro died. The pet doctors even marveled at his behaviour, pampering Riro warmly as if it was human. Riro gave up the ghost at the veterinary center. Dara carried his dead weeping as if a great disaster has befallen him. He could hardly hide his feelings. He could not suppress his emotions as more and more water ran his jest. Obviously, he wore his heart on his sleeves.v

CHAPTER 15

Picture 5 Here

When Dara arrived at the front of their building, he stood still. Sympathizers watched him with pity. He lifted Riro in his hand - Dead trunk. Apart from the stain, his shirt was drenched with tears. Instinctive gush of sweat has a fill of his outer skin layer, at the various parts of his body. Though this flow was at a reduced rate as at this period. The stench from his blood-defaced

T-shirt has already attracted the throng of flies which wrestled to gain hold of him.

Teenagers and children sympathizers who could no longer withhold their emotions burst in tears in commiseration.

His lips motioned consistently without muffling any word. He stood still, hallucinating the events of the adorable days of Riro on his survival quest. He could remember this generous partner whose sons and daughters were disposed for him to keep the schooling dreams alive. A partner who made it easy for him to manage the difficulties of being an orphan and, deserted. A true friend at points of troubles. May be for once now, the boy would succumb to reckon with the saying that "Life is too mathematical than the mathematicians. You could only figure out how to approach it. You might never be able to dictate the elements that sum it all."

Now with Riro's death, his calculation about exam fee payment was way off beam. He has nowhere in particular at heart to start life over again.

Dara could obviously see the END written in bold letters. Riro's fatality was too fatal to his ambitions. He looked like the most miserable of all men. It was glaring that his fetching handsomeness has disappeared in his sobbing cry. As he took a step forward after the long pause in movement, Dara fetched a deep sigh again and lifted his voice in agony of passion.

" Riro o o o o o!' He screamed as if the dog could hear his voice wherever her spirit might be, and wagged her tail as of the good old days.

This is but a dead-end!

Let the rain falls

But no amount of it,

Could wash away my tears.

My mouth is bitter

Like a vine gall.

My spirit is sorrowful

Even unto death.

Riro! Riro!! Riro!!!

In bad order you left things

For me alone to carry on.

How do I live hence

In your absence?

Who will in your instead,

Bodyguard me by the day?

Where is my watcher

At the dead of the night?

Who shall kiss my plate

Of meal with me from now?

Who could subdue

My loneliness like you?

How do I maintain

My gazelle-swiftness

When you are no more?

Who acts on, your parts

On my chosen career?

Who rescue me again

In the rivers of stoppage?

Riro! Will this life

Ever continues without you?

My history without you

Will be a frame up!"

After his lament, Dara buried the corpse and inscribed verses on her tombstone in reminiscence of the dog's faithful companionship. The epitaph read:

MY BELOVED

The only one that was there

When Papa was no longer alive.

No one else, but you cared for me.

The one who felt as I felt.

My nurse and my companion.

Like the sun suddenly disappeared

When you walked out of my life

To make life a boring place

For me to live hence.

I stand before the sun

To declare my love for you;

As you did love me

With your heart and soul.

I would have joined you

On this unpleasant journey;

But fate says we shall

Never take the same route;

For a man's spirit goes

Upward when he dies

And the spirit of the beast

Goes down to the earth.

How I wish our re-union again;

Sometime when this life is over.

Oh! My lover, my ever Riro.

My soul shall pant for you always!

"My helpmate."

Picture 6 Here

Dara eventually rose up from the base of the tomb after several failed effort to console him. The whole world bore witness he was sorrowful. He appeared tattered, haggard and destabilized. Riro's demise was as an eye-injury. Irresistibly, the sun that rose in the east and set in the west on this day was to his disfavour. To him, fate was a bad master. Why would fulfilment resolve to keep him at bay? Every one knew Riro was the surviving bedrock of his aspiration. Besides, here was a boy who wrote no epitaph on his father's tomb, but in respect of a beast, his heart flopped. His eyes never ceased to shed tears. His taut mouth was muted as if he should say no word again till eternity.

He drew the curtain of their parlor to prevent the on lookers who said:

'His helpmate."

'The Helpmate'

The song: I must grow in all my day to day

In every departments

Endeavors of my life.

I must grow in all my day to day

In every departments

I shall not remain same.

The sofa: s : d. m: d. m m. r. d. L:

s. f. f: m. r. D:

d. s, s. m. f. R:

s; f. m:d; m,m.r.d.l:

s. f, f. m, r. D:

S. m, m. t. r. D:

Words List

Argy-bargy(n): noisy but not serious quarrelling.

Bawdily(adv): amusing in a coarse or indecent way

Bawled(v): shout or cry loudly

Bay(n): into a position from which escape is impossible

Befuddled(adj): make stupid or confused

Bitch(n): a female dog

Chamber(n): a room (especially) a bedroom.

Cuticle(n): skin at the base of a finger or toe-nail

Cynosure(n) : someone or something that has become attention or admiration.

Delinquency(n) : petty crime committed by young people.

Derogatory(adj) : showing a critical attitude or expressing bad behavior.

Dilapidated(v) : something falling to pieces or that which is in a bad state of repair.

Discomfitted(adj): to be confused and embarrassed

Downpour : heavy and unusual sudden fall of rain.

Fangs(n): long sharp tooth, esp. of Dogs

Farinaceous(adj): starchy or floury e.g bread

Fastidious(adj): selecting carefully

Floundering(v): struggle helplessly or clumsily

Growled(v): make a low threatening sound

Gutsy(adj): full of courage & determination

Guzzle(v): eat or drink greedily

Hallucinate(v): imaging one is seeing or hearing when no such thing is present

Haunches(n): the fleshy part of the buttocks

Idiosyncrasy(n): a behaviour pattern

Instinct : a tendency that one is born with to behave in a certain way without reasoning or training.

Kindred : a family relation.

Matey(adj): sociable; familiar; friendly

Perturbation : an instance of being very worried.

Premonition: a feeling that something is going to happen, especially unpleasant thing.

Prickly(adv): of a person, easily angered

Reminiscence(n): recalling of past events & experiences

Scuffle(n) : a confused struggle between people who are close together.

Spontaneous(adj) : an action or reaction done as a result of sudden impulse from within.

Strain(n): condition of being stretched

Straitened circumstances(n): having scarcely enough money to live on; in poverty

Strand(n): sandy shores of a river

Summer(n) : the warmest season of the year, coming between spring and autumn.

Winter(n) : the last and coldest season of the year. (Winter lasts from December to February in the Northern parts of the world).

Vicinity(n) : the area round a place.

Practice Questions

(1) The difficulties reached the climax when the poor Papa died; which difficulties? Explain.

(2 The use of the 'brilliant sun' in chapter 1, page 1; what figure of speech is expressed here? (a) Metaphor(b) Personification

(3) "The brilliant sun refused to shine, paleness bothered the sky. Nothing made serious meanings like the beginning of an end. Wearable surroundings. The lookers-on loitered compassion; it was papa's interment." The lines as contained in page 1 seem to indicate the nature's concerns for the unfortunate incident of papa's death. What figure of speech is demonstrated by this expression?

   (a) Simile   (b) Pathetic Fallacy

(4) " . . . but for this boy. How would Dara survive? . . . how would he continue his education?" Does time eventually supplies answers to these rhetorical questions? If yes, how?

(5) "while he was in money, his household still suffered." Whom was this line referring to?

(6) What engineered the divorce between Papa and his wife?

(7 "It was an open secret that Papa died of venereal diseases". What figure of speech is demonstrated with the word "open secret"?   (a) Hyperbole (b) Oxymoron.

(8 Papa's burial was a disappointment, judging by the story line. What are the reasons responsible for his wretched burial?

9) "They all have battalions back home to fend for." whom were the author referring to as battalions?

(10) "His mother left Papa when . . . ?" Complete the statement.

(11) Why do you think Dara would be disappointed trying to conceive any of the sympathizers at papa's interment for assistance?

(12) "Dara bought this bitch while he was in class one . . ." which bitch?

(13) " . . . Dara was weeping as he observe Papa lifted into the final carriage of all living" What was the author referring to as final carriage?

(14) "Dara said this prayer solemnly every morning" which prayer?

(15) Mr. Mali and Bro. Okonkwo are two children friendly elders in the course of the story. What different influential roles do they play in the lives of the kids? Why was one accepted and the other viewed as a disturbance?

(16) Mr. Akin was frustrated because Solo turned out a spoilt child. Who spoilt him and how?

(17) Why do you think Babaijesha has problem with being called Daddy? What was his literal meaning of the common name 'Daddy' as a Yoruba man?

(18) Why do you think Mr. Dauda enjoyed working with Dara?

(19) The desire for recognition landed Dara in an offensive situation should the villagers see him in their river. How did Riro came into the picture in this situation and what magic did she perform?

20) Did Dara actually have an helpmate and what was his helpmate?

(21) What significance is the use of 'her' and 'she' for Riro in the story?

(22) On typical occasions, Dara failed to reciprocate Riro's affection in practical actions. Where and when?

(23) "That would be an easy calamity . . ." The word easy calamity in page 47, paragraph 2 in the story line suggests the use of: (a) Oxymoron (b) Hyperbole

(24) In the course of Dara's survival, what role did persistency and relentlessness play and, how relevant could these terms be, reviewing the present predicament of Dara, especially after Riro's demise?

www.ingramcontent.com/pod-product-compliance
Lightning Source LLC
Chambersburg PA
CBHW051227120626
46547CB00013B/1544